THIS FAMILY OF OURS

A KEEPSAKE JOURNAL

ANNE PHYFE PALMER

ILLUSTRATED BY SARAH TRUMBAUER

SASQUATCH BOOKS
SEATTLE

W0019314

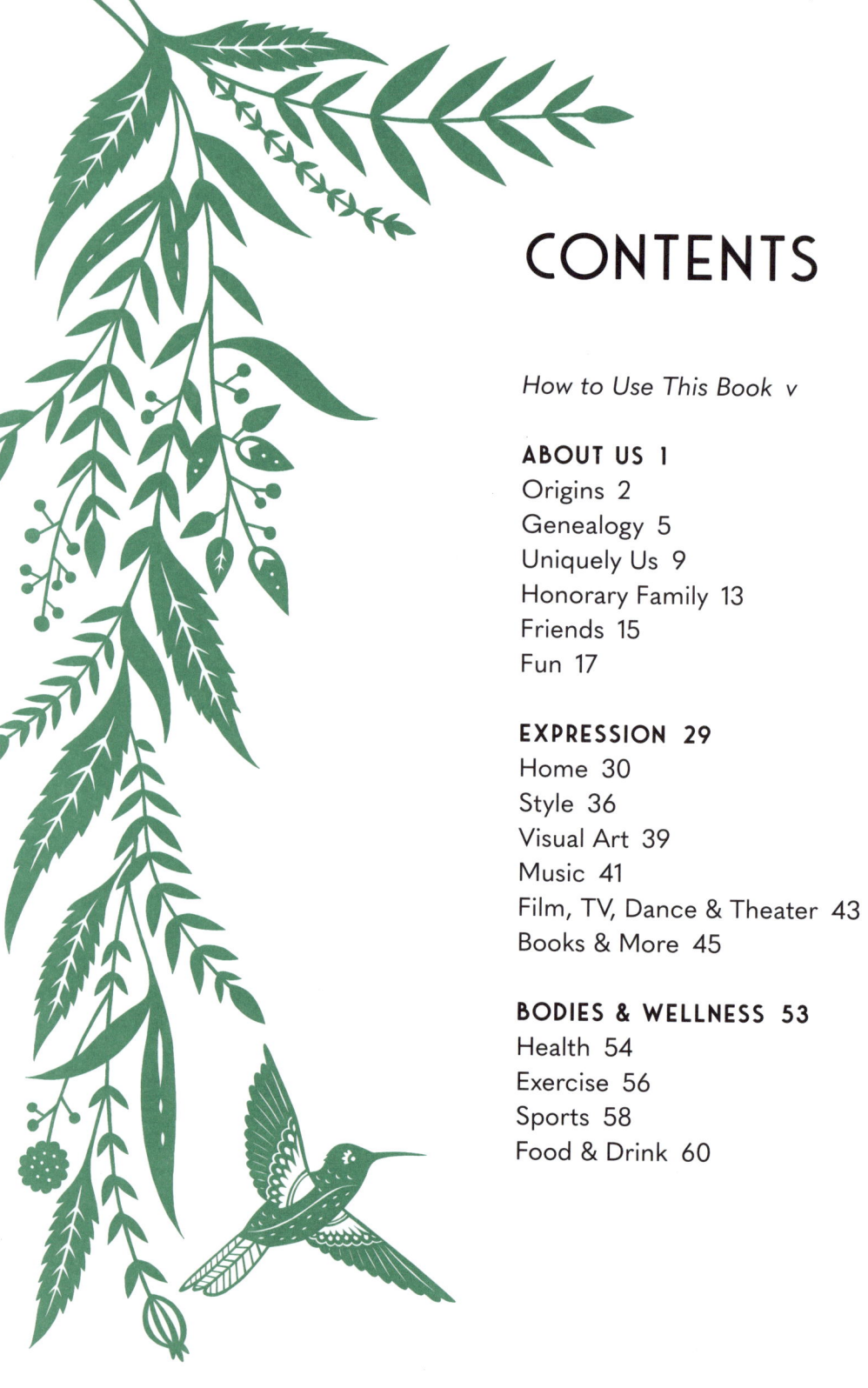

CONTENTS

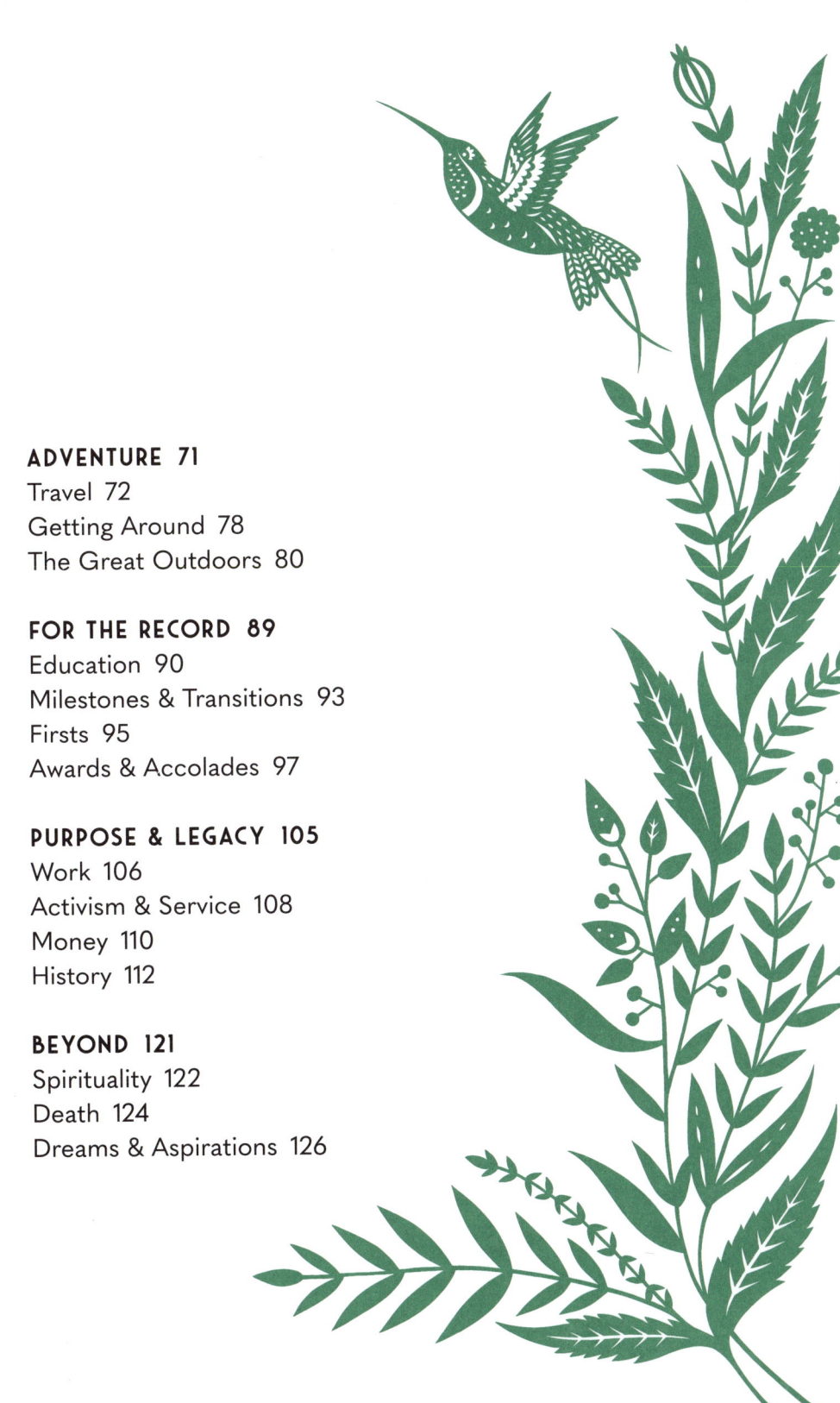

HOW TO USE
THIS BOOK

This book was designed for families of all kinds to record the facts, details, experiences, and plans of their commingled lives. Here are some tips for getting the most out of this journal:

1. Designate one person as the main recorder, but find a way for each family member to contribute.

2. Keep your journal somewhere accessible to the whole family for easy additions.

3. Tackle the group questions on a road trip or a family vacation, or when you have time to relax together; writing takes brain energy, especially writing that involves remembering and making choices!

4. Skip questions for later if they are holding you up.

5. Allow your family to take several passes at each section. You might find it helpful to jump around and answer just a few questions from each section in one sitting.

6. Use the "More to Know" pages after each section to write more, or to add your own prompts and family information.

7. Revisit and add to this journal at least once a year.

ABOUT US

ORIGINS

What the word *family* means to us: ....
....
....
....
....
....
....
....
....

Our family in six words: ....
....
....
....
....
....

Our origin story: ....
....
....
....
....
....
....
....
....
....
....
....
....
....
....
....
....
....
....
....

Family members and when/where they were born: ....

....

....

....

....

....

....

....

....

....

The significance of our names: ....

....

....

....

....

....

....

....

....

....

GENEALOGY

What we know about our genealogy: ....
....
....
....
....
....
....
....
....
....
....
....
....
....
....
....
....
....

Our family tree:

Grandparents and where they are from and where they live: ....

....

....

....

....

....

....

....

....

....

Aunts and uncles and where they live: ....

....

....

....

....

....

....

....

....

....

Cousins: ....

....

....

....

....

....

....

....

....

....

....

....

....

....

UNIQUELY US

What it's like to be in this family: ....

....

....

....

....

....

....

....

....

What makes us unique: ....

....

....

....

....

....

....

....

What we like to talk and learn about: ....

....

....

....

....

....

....

....

....

....

Common sayings in our family: ....

....

....

....

....

....

....

....

....

A few remarkable details about our history: ....
....
....
....
....
....
....
....
....
....
....
....
....
....
....
....
....
....

Rituals or traditions in our family: ....

....

....

....

....

....

....

....

....

....

....

....

....

....

....

....

....

....

HONORARY FAMILY

Our pets and/or favorite animals: ....
....
....
....
....
....
....
....
....
....

Memorable babysitters or caretakers: ....
....
....
....
....
....
....
....
....

Honorary family members: ....

....

....

....

....

....

....

....

....

....

....

....

....

....

....

FRIENDS

Our closest family friends: ....

....

....

....

....

....

....

....

Closest friends of each member of the family: ....

....

....

....

....

....

....

....

....

Friends who have really come through for us: ....
....
....
....
....
....
....
....
....

Close neighbors: ....
....
....
....
....
....
....
....

FUN

What we do to have fun: ....
....
....
....
....
....
....
....
....
....
....
....
....
....
....
....

Ways we celebrate: ....
....
....
....
....
....
....
....
....
....

Parties or events we have hosted: ....
....
....
....
....
....
....
....
....
....

Our hobbies and ones we would like to explore: ....

....

....

....

....

....

....

....

....

....

....

....

....

....

....

....

....

....

....

....

Games we play: ....
....
....
....
....
....
....
....
....

Special parties or events we have attended: ....
....
....
....
....
....
....
....
....

Holidays or annual celebrations we mark: ....

....

....

....

....

....

....

....

....

....

....

....

Ways we enjoy spending time with others: ....

....

....

....

....

....

....

....

....

....

Groups or clubs we are a part of: ....

....

....

....

....

....

....

....

....

....

....

How we entertain ourselves on a rainy day: ....

....

....

....

....

....

....

....

....

....

....

....

A time we laughed so hard our stomachs hurt: ....
....
....
....
....
....
....
....
....
....
....
....
....
....
....
....
....

MORE TO KNOW

....
....
....
....
....
....
....
....
....
....
....
....
....
....

HOME

We have lived in these neighborhoods, cities, states, and countries: ....

....

....

....

....

....

....

....

....

....

....

The kinds of homes we have lived in: ....

....

....

....

....

....

....

One of our homes looked like this:

Beloved objects and the stories behind them: ....

....

....

....

....

....

....

A favorite piece of furniture: ....

....

....

....

Heirlooms that have been passed down and the stories behind them: ....

....

....

....

....

....

....

A drawing or description of a room in a family home

and something that took place there:

The style or architecture in one of our favorite homes: ....

....

....

....

....

....

....

....

People tend to gather in this/these room(s): ....

....

....

....

....

....

....

....

Best place to read or write: ....

....

....

....

....

....

....

Best place to take a nap: ....

....

....

....

....

....

....

In our neighborhood there is: ....

....

....

....

....

....

The hub of our neighborhood is: ....

....

....

....

....

....

....

STYLE

Our overall family style is: ....

....

....

....

....

....

....

....

Our style, by family member, and how it may have evolved: ....

....

....

....

....

....

....

....

....

Particular outfit each of us is known for: ....

....

....

....

....

....

....

....

....

....

What we wear around the house: ....

....

....

....

....

....

....

What dressing up means in our family: ....

....

....

....

....

....

....

Hairstyles or accessories we have worn: ....

....

....

....

....

VISUAL ART

Types of art our family creates: ....
....
....
....
....
....
....

Art and artists we appreciate or enjoy: ....
....
....
....
....
....
....
....
....
....
....
....
....

Art classes we have taken or taught: ....

....

....

....

....

....

Art in our home and its meaning: ....

....

....

....

....

Museums or public art we have visited: ....

....

....

....

....

....

....

MUSIC

Instruments we play/enjoy: ....
....
....
....
....

Musical genres we enjoy: ....
....
....
....
....
....

Musicians we like: ....
....
....
....
....
....

This album/these songs make up the soundtrack of our family: ....

....

....

....

....

....

....

....

....

First concert we attended together: ....

....

....

Other concerts or festivals we have attended, together or not: ....

....

....

....

....

....

....

....

FILM, TV, DANCE & THEATER

Movies we have enjoyed together: ....
....
....
....
....
....
....

TV shows we have enjoyed together: ....
....
....
....
....
....
....

Performances we have enjoyed together: ....

....

....

....

....

....

....

....

....

Performances we have participated in or supported: ....

....

....

....

....

....

....

....

....

BOOKS & MORE

Our favorite authors: ....

....

....

....

....

....

....

....

Our favorite children's books: ....

....

....

....

....

....

....

....

Books, magazines, or other publications that are important to us:

....

....

....

....

....

....

....

....

....

If someone wrote a book about our family, it would be called: ....

....

....

A book that reminds us of our family: ....

....

....

Poets we enjoy: ....

....

....

....

A poem we love:

MORE TO KNOW

....
....
....
....
....
....
....
....
....
....
....
....
....
....

BODIES & WELLNESS

HEALTH

Our healthcare providers over the years: ....

....

....

....

....

Our dental care providers: ....

....

....

....

....

Minor illnesses or injuries: ....

....

....

....

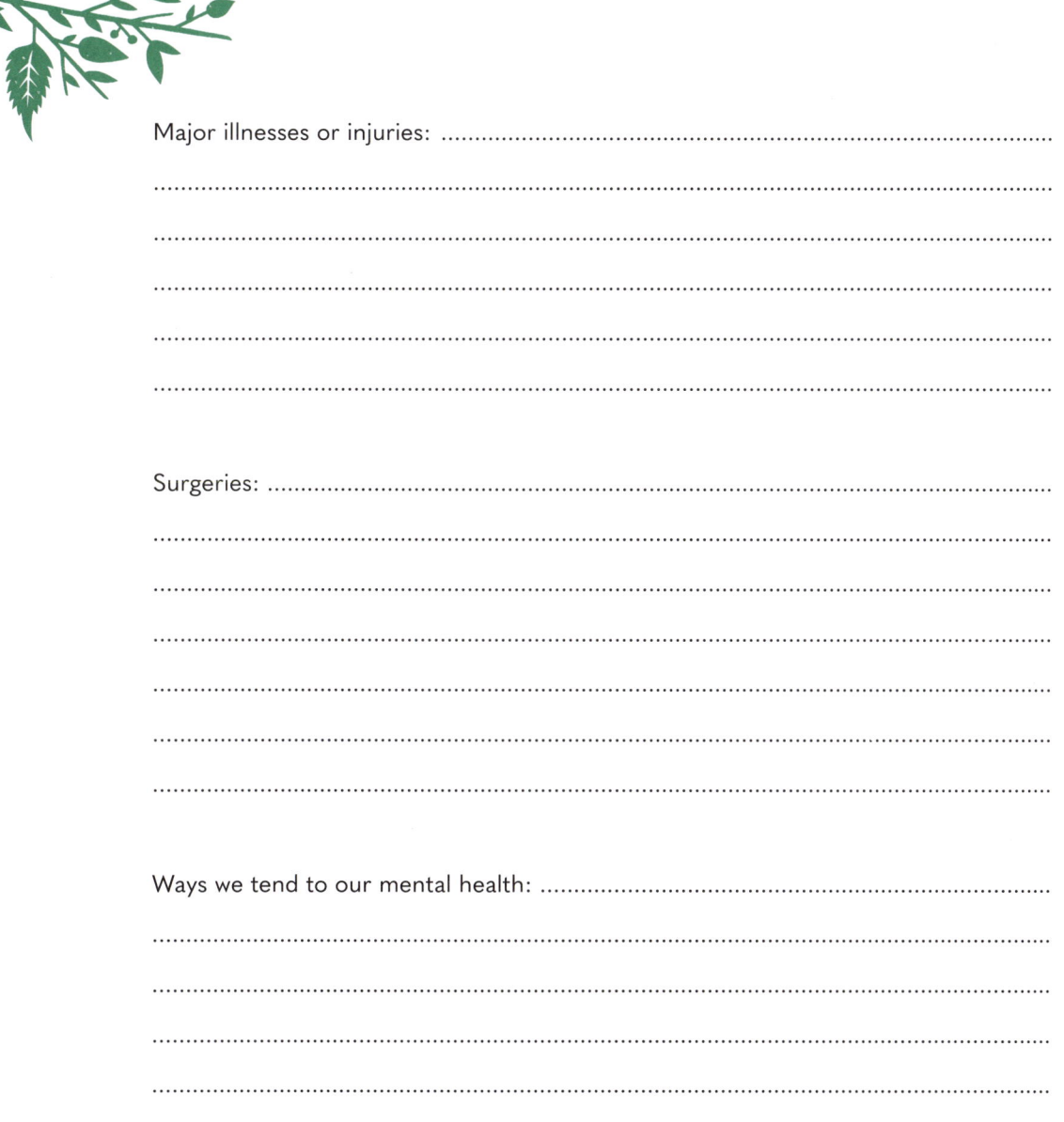

Major illnesses or injuries: ....

....

....

....

....

....

Surgeries: ....

....

....

....

....

....

....

Ways we tend to our mental health: ....

....

....

....

....

....

EXERCISE

Ways we exercise as a family: ....
....
....
....
....
....
....

Ways we exercise individually: ....
....
....
....
....
....
....

Why we exercise: ....
....
....
....
....
....
....

Gyms, community centers, or studios we attend: ....
....
....
....
....
....
....

Walks we take around our home: ....
....
....
....
....
....
....

SPORTS

Sports we like to play: ....

....

....

....

....

....

....

....

Sports we like to watch: ....

....

....

....

....

....

....

....

....

....

Teams we root for: ....
....
....
....
....
....
....
....
....

Our favorite athletes: ....
....
....
....
....
....
....
....

FOOD & DRINK

Our favorite foods: ....
....
....
....
....
....
....
....
....

We never eat: ....
....
....
....
....

Our favorite snack foods: ....
....
....
....

Cereals in the cupboard: ....
....
....
....
....

Food and drinks we associate with events or holidays: ....
....
....
....
....
....
....
....
....

Some meaningful meals we have shared: ....
....
....
....
....

Foods we like to make together: ....
....
....
....
....
....
....
....
....
....

When we eat together, we: ....
....
....
....
....
....
....

When we invite guests for dinner, we like to make: ....

....

....

....

....

....

....

....

....

....

Our favorite places to eat away from home: ....

....

....

....

....

....

....

....

A few favorite family recipes:

MORE TO KNOW

....

....

....

....

....

....

....

....

....

....

....

....

....

....

....

TRAVEL

Our most memorable trips and why: ....
....
....
....
....
....
....
....
....
....
....
....
....
....
....
....

Quintessential family vacation(s): ....
....
....
....
....
....
....
....
....
....

Places we would like to visit: ....
....
....
....
....
....
....
....
....
....

A log of our top five adventures: ....

....

....

....

....

....

....

....

....

....

....

....

....

....

....

....

....

....

....

....

....

....

....
....
....
....
....
....
....
....
....
....
....
....
....
....
....
....

GETTING AROUND

How we get around our town or city: ....
....
....
....
....
....
....
....

First family vehicle: ....
....
....

Our favorite bicycle adventures: ....
....
....
....
....
....
....
....

Best road trip: ....
....
....
....
....
....

A time we got lost: ....
....
....
....

Memorable experiences by bus, train, plane, or boat: ....
....
....
....
....
....
....

THE GREAT OUTDOORS

Our favorite places in nature: ....
....
....
....
....
....

National parks or wilderness areas we have visited: ....
....
....
....
....
....

Our greatest outdoor adventure: ....
....
....
....
....
....

Our favorite local parks and playgrounds: ....
....
....
....
....
....

Our favorite hikes: ....
....
....
....
....

Places we swim: ....
....
....
....
....

Rivers, lakes, and oceans we have floated or boated on: ....
....
....
....

In the winter, we: ....
....
....
....
....
....
....
....
....

When spring arrives, we: ....
....
....
....
....
....
....
....
....

What summers are like: ....
....
....
....
....
....
....
....

Our favorite fall rituals or activities: ....
....
....
....
....
....
....
....

MORE TO KNOW

....
....
....
....
....
....
....
....
....
....
....
....
....
....
....

FOR THE RECORD

EDUCATION

Where we have attended school: ....

....

....

....

....

....

....

....

....

Post–high school education, training, or degrees: ....

....

....

....

....

....

....

....

....

Most memorable teachers, mentors, and coaches: ....
....
....
....
....
....
....
....

Subjects we loved: ....
....
....
....
....
....
....
....

Learning outside of school: ....

....

....

....

....

....

....

....

....

....

....

....

....

....

....

....

....

....

MILESTONES & TRANSITIONS

Births: ....
....
....
....

Graduations: ....
....
....
....
....

Weddings: ....
....
....
....

Promotions: ....
....
....

Deaths: ....
....
....
....
....
....

More milestones and transitions: ....
....
....
....
....
....
....
....
....
....
....
....

FIRSTS

Tooth: ....
....
....
....

Lost tooth: ....
....
....
....

Job: ....
....
....
....

Date: ....
....
....
....

Drive: ....

....

....

....

First _____ : ....

....

....

....

First _____ : ....

....

....

....

First _____ : ....

....

....

....

AWARDS & ACCOLADES

School: ....
....
....
....

Work: ....
....
....
....

Arts and sciences: ....
....
....

Sports: ....
....
....

Civic/community: ....
....
....

More awards and accolades:

MORE TO KNOW

....
....
....
....
....
....
....
....
....
....
....
....
....
....

PURPOSE & LEGACY

WORK

Jobs the kids have had: ....
....
....
....
....
....
....

Jobs the adults have had: ....
....
....
....
....
....
....

Most interesting qualifications on our resumes: ....

....

....

....

....

....

Jobs or work that have been most meaningful: ....

....

....

....

....

....

....

Housework each of us does: ....

....

....

....

....

....

ACTIVISM & SERVICE

Causes that mean the most to us: ....
....
....
....
....
....
....

Community service or activism our family does: ....
....
....
....
....
....
....

Marches or protests we have attended: ....
....
....
....
....

Political or ideological campaigns we have supported: ....
....
....
....
....

Family members who have served in the military, and how: ....
....
....
....
....

Family members who have died in a conflict: ....
....
....
....
....

MONEY

Our family philosophy on money: ....
....
....
....
....
....
....
....
....

How we manage our finances: ....
....
....
....
....
....
....
....
....

How we teach our kids the value of money: ....
....
....
....
....
....
....
....
....
....
....

How our kids earn money: ....
....
....
....
....
....
....
....

HISTORY

How historical events have impacted our family: ....

....

....

....

....

....

....

....

....

....

The greatest hardship our family has endured: ....

....

....

....

....

....

....

The most repeated family story: ....

....

....

....

....

....

....

....

....

....

....

....

....

....

....

....

One of the great love stories in our family: ....

....

....

....

....

....

....

....

....

....

....

....

....

....

....

....

....

....

Major world events that our family has witnessed or experienced: ....

....

....

....

....

....

....

....

....

....

....

....

....

....

....

....

....

....

....

....

....

MORE TO KNOW

....

....

....

....

....

....

....

....

....

....

....

....

....

....

SPIRITUALITY

Our family's spiritual/religious inclination: ....
....
....
....
....

Practices and/or rituals we engage in: ....
....
....
....
....

Our favorite spiritual quotes or scriptures: ....
....
....
....
....
....
....

Significant events and celebrations in our spiritual practices: ....

....

....

....

....

....

....

....

....

....

....

....

....

....

....

DEATH

Loved ones who have passed away: ....

....

....

....

....

....

....

....

Animals we have lost: ....

....

....

....

....

Funerals we have attended: ....

....

....

....

....

Ways we have celebrated the life of someone we have lost: ....

....

....

....

....

....

What we believe happens when we die: ....

....

....

....

....

....

....

....

....

DREAMS & ASPIRATIONS

Our long-term dreams and aspirations: ....
....
....
....
....
....
....
....
....
....
....
....
....
....
....
....
....

Aspirational stories in our family: ....
....
....
....
....
....
....
....
....
....
....
....
....
....
....
....
....
....
....
....
....

Our family's annual goals for the future:

YEAR: _____

....

....

....

....

....

....

....

....

....

....

....

....

....

....

....

....

....

YEAR: _____

....
....
....
....
....
....
....
....
....
....
....
....
....
....
....
....
....

YEAR: _____

....
....
....
....
....
....
....
....
....
....
....
....
....
....

YEAR: _____

YEAR: _____

YEAR: _____

....
....
....
....
....
....
....
....
....
....
....
....
....
....
....

YEAR: _____

....
....
....
....
....
....
....
....
....
....
....
....
....
....
....
....
....
....
....

YEAR: _____

....
....
....
....
....
....
....
....
....
....
....
....
....
....
....
....
....
....

ABOUT THE AUTHOR

ANNE PHYFE PALMER is an entrepreneur, writer, yoga teacher, sailor, and electric bike–commuter who left her hometown of New Orleans and founded 8 Limbs Yoga Centers in Seattle. With her guided journal series from Sasquatch, Anne Phyfe takes her passion for personal inquiry from the yoga mat to the written word. She lives in Seattle with her family. You can find her at AnnePhyfe.com. *PS: Anne Phyfe is her first name!*

ABOUT THE ARTIST

SARAH TRUMBAUER is a papercut artist and illustrator living in rural eastern Pennsylvania. Her paper cuts are inspired by long walks through gardens, vintage children's books, and art nouveau patterns. Her work has been featured in international magazines, books, and stationery products. When she's not cutting paper, she can be found drinking tea, daydreaming, and reading mystery novels with her cat, Lucy.

Copyright © 2021 by Anne Phyfe Palmer

All rights reserved. No portion of this book may be reproduced or utilized
in any form, or by any electronic, mechanical, or other means, without the
prior written permission of the publisher.

Printed in Colombia

SASQUATCH BOOKS with colophon is a registered trademark
of Blue Star Press, LLC

29 28 27 26 25   9 8 7 6 5 4 3 2

Editor: Susan Roxborough | Production editor: Bridget Sweet
Design: Anna Goldstein and Alison Keefe | Illustrations: Sarah Trumbauer

ISBN: 978-1-63217-379-9

Sasquatch Books | 1325 Fourth Avenue, Suite 1025 | Seattle, WA 98101

SasquatchBooks.com